TABLE OF CONTENTS

KU-350-965

Unless otherwise indicated, all Scripture quotations are taken from the King James Version of the Bible.
Unstoppable Passion · ISBN 1-56394-296-8/B-224
Copyright © 2007 by *MIKE MURDOCK*
All publishing rights belong exclusively to Wisdom International
Publisher/Editor: Deborah Murdock Johnson
Published by The Wisdom Center · 4051 Denton Highway · Fort Worth, Texas 76117
1-817-759-BOOK · 1-817-759-0300
You Will Love Our Website...! www.TheWisdomCenter.tv

Accuracy Department: To our Friends and Partners...We welcome any comments on errors or misprints you find in our book...Email our department: AccuracyDept@thewisdomcenter.tv. Your aid in helping us excel is highly valued.

You Will Only
Be Remembered
For Your Obsession.

-MIKE MURDOCK

≈ **1** ≈

PASSION IS WHEN YOUR GOAL BECOMES YOUR ONLY OBSESSION

You Will Never Have Significant Success With Anything Until It Becomes An Obsession With You.

15 Facts About Passion

1. Passion Is An Excessive And Uncommon Desire. An *obsession* is when something *consumes* your thoughts and time. It includes the desire to change, produce or achieve a *specific* goal.

2. Passion Is The Power That Decides Your Life Legacy. *You Will Only Be Remembered In Your Life For Your Obsession.* Henry Ford is remembered for the automobile. Thomas Edison... inventions. Billy Graham...evangelism. Oral Roberts...healing. The Wright brothers...the airplane.

3. Jesus Revealed His Own Passion For His Mission And Goal In Life. "For the Son of man is come to seek and to save that which was lost," (Luke 19:10). The Father revealed His own passion and love for us through the healing power of Jesus. "How God anointed Jesus of Nazareth with the Holy Ghost and with power: Who went about doing good, and healing all that were oppressed of the devil; for God was with Him," (Acts 10:38).

4.   Jesus Acknowledged The Importance Of Our Passion To Pursue And Know God. "Jesus said unto him, Thou shalt love the Lord thy God with all thy heart, and with all thy soul, and with all thy mind.   This is the first and great commandment," (Matthew 22:37-38).

Passion reaches. Passion invests The Currency of Time. Reaching is a Signal. Are you truly hungry for a relationship with your Heavenly Father?   Then, remember…The Price Of God's Presence Is Time.

Move toward His presence today.   *Habitually* schedule time in The Secret Place. "He that dwelleth in the secret place of the most High shall abide under the shadow of the Almighty," (Psalm 91:1).   *In His Presence* your passion for Him will grow from a *tiny acorn* to a *huge oak* within you.

5.   The Proof Of Passion Is Pursuit.   A woman told me one time, "Oh, I wish I could play the piano like you."

I said, "Oh, so are you taking lessons?"

She said, "No."

I asked, "Do you *own* a piano?"

She said, "No."

I said, "Are you going to *buy* a piano?"

She replied, "No."

I teasingly said, "Then, you lie!"

The Proof Of Passion Is Pursuit.

I have always loved saxophone music.   So, I always told everybody, "Oh, I *wish* I could play a saxophone."   I said it for years.

One day, I felt the inner, quiet voice of The Holy Spirit whisper to me, "Take lessons."

I was a bit indignant, "I don't want to."

"Shut up, then." *(It's hard to believe The Spirit can be that direct, but He was!)*

6.   The Family Of God Is Instructed To Develop A Passion For The Word Of God. The Lord spoke to Joshua about the Law and instructed him to "...turn not from it to the right hand or to the left, that thou mayest prosper whithersoever thou goest. This book of the law shall not depart out of thy mouth; but thou shalt meditate therein day and night, that thou mayest observe to do according to all that is written therein: for then thou shalt make thy way prosperous, and then thou shalt have good success," (Joshua 1:7-8). Oh, ask The Father to birth a craving and hunger for His Word! You cannot survive the adversarial environment of Earth without the inner strength of His Words within you.

7.   Passion   Requires   A   Sacrificial Lifestyle. The famed world evangelist, Billy Graham spoke all over the world. That required him to be away from his family for several months at a time. Why? *Passion. His wife's passion* for God enabled her to *endure* it. I like what she said. They asked Ruth, "How did you feel about having to raise your children alone while your husband, Billy Graham, stayed gone from your home to preach the gospel?" She said that she would rather have the *slice* of a great man than the *whole* of an average man! That is passion...for the Will of God.

8.   Passion Is Revealed By How Much Energy And Time You Are Willing To Invest. *The Price Of Your Future Is The Exchange Of Something In Your Present.* "Whatsoever thy hand findeth to do, do it with thy might; for there is no work, nor device, nor knowledge, nor wisdom, in the grave, whither thou goest," (Ecclesiastes 9:10).

Your Focus Determines Your Feelings.

9. Passion Decides Your Ability To Endure Attack And Opposition. *Persuasion Decides Endurance.* Throughout Scripture, the passion of believers sustained them through seasons of severe persecution. People tried to kill Charles Wesley, the great Methodist preacher, the brother of John Wesley. I read once that he had to hide for months. His Persuasions created his passion.

10. Your Passion Can Choose A Wrong Focus. Terrorists have a passion to destroy, to create pain and loss. Why? Somewhere, at some point in their experiences with humans, they felt disrespected. So, it is important that the passion of your life has the *right* focus. Your Focus IS...your World. Wisdom Key: *Your Chosen Focus Is The World You Have Created For Yourself.*

11. Passion Can Be Misused. Passion is not necessarily the proof of *Greatness.* Hitler had passion and created the Holocaust, the murder of millions of Jews. *Passion simply reveals persuasion...not greatness.* Yes, great men usually possess uncommon passion, but so do evil men! *Passion is energy.* It is something you believe.

12. Passion Is Necessary For You To Find God. God is not *accidentally* discovered. He requires passionate pursuit. Listen to what Jeremiah 29:13 says, "And ye shall seek Me, and find Me, *when* ye shall search for Me *with all your heart." The Intensity Of Your Passion Decides What You Discover.*

13. It Is Your Personal Responsibility To Protect The Smallest Scent Of Passion Within You. Others are often self-absorbed, unfeeling of your needs, beliefs and deep concerns. Passion begins as a tiny Seed. *Water* it. *Guard* it. *Grow* it. Be immovable.

Keys to protecting your passion include visualizing your Future (Goal) so big that yesterday dies. Four enemies of Passion include: fatigue, busyness, over-scheduling and disrespectful relationships.

14. Your Passion Can Make You Unforgettable. That is why Jesus Christ continues to affect the daily life of millions 2,000 years after His Death and Resurrection. Jesus focused on doing the *precise* instructions of His Heavenly Father. He *healed* the sick. He *comforted* the lonely. He came to *mend* the broken, *lift* the fallen and *teach* the unlearned.

15. Pursuing Your Passion May Cost You Everything You Own. Consider Jesus! The passion of Jesus took Him to the cross. It took Him to the crucifixion. *Eight-inch thorns* were crushed into His brow. A *spear* punctured His side. *Spikes* were driven into His hands. Thirty-nine stripes of a *whip* tore His back to shreds. Four hundred soldiers *spat* upon His body. His beard was *ripped* off His face.

Yet, *He was obsessed with the salvation of mankind.* And He succeeded.

Passion is always...always...costly.

Passion Is When Your Goal Becomes Your Only Obsession.

Uncommon Men Have
Uncommon Passion.

-MIKE MURDOCK

2

Passion Turns Common Men Into Uncommon Men

Passion Is The Difference Between Humans.
Michael Korda, senior editor of *Time Magazine,* once wrote in his book, *Success,* that *the number one ingredient for success is energy. Energy.* Passion is what distinguishes Tiger Woods from a thousand other golfers, and Michael Jordan from a thousand other basketball players. Passion is a treasured commodity.

Uncommon Men Have Uncommon Passion. That is why the young warrior shepherd David ran toward his enemy, Goliath. He celebrated his victories with the same intense passion. (See 2 Samuel 6:14.)

The Proof Of Passion Is The Investment Of Time. Uncommon legendary sportsmen prove their passion by *their investment of time. Larry Bird,* the basketball legend, practiced 500 free throws before breakfast every morning. *Shaquille O'Neal,* the famed basketball star, shot free throws every night from 7:30 to 8:30. Famed golfer, *Tiger Woods* was on the golf course at 4:30 a.m., believe it or not, with his father *when he was two and one-half years old!*

Passion Creates Legends. One of my favorite people in the world is Muhammad Ali. I had the wonderful privilege of spending a couple of days in the same hotel with him and meeting him many years ago. I found him *brilliant, articulate* and *passionate.* His outspokenness and passion alienated some people, but he lived his persuasion every single day. Muhammad Ali used to get up early every morning for arduous hard road work training.

Passion Distinguishes Olympic Champions From The Rest Of The World.

Passion was the invisible volcano hidden inside Lance Armstrong who overcame cancer to become the greatest cyclist in the world. The Old Testament Prophet *Isaiah was the Picture of Passion.* *"Therefore have I set my face like a flint,* and I know that I shall not be ashamed,"* (Isaiah 50:7). Tonight, Fox News Commentator Bill O'Reilly asked a question of the famed singer, Smokey Robinson. O'Reilly asked him to explain his incredible longevity in the music industry. Smokey replied simply, *"I have a passion for what I do."*

Passion Turns Common Ministers Into Uncommon Ministers. The Apostle Paul was truly an uncommon voice that penetrated the known world in his day. His words still burn like a branding torch: "...this one thing I do,...*I press toward the mark for the prize of the high calling of God in Christ Jesus,"* (Philippians 3:13-14).

Completing Your Assignment On The Earth Will Require Uncommon Passion. Jesus had such passion. "Who for the joy that was set before Him endured the cross, despising the shame, and is set down at the right hand of the throne of God," (Hebrews 12:2; also read Hebrew 12:3).

Uncommon Success Is Always Accompanied By Uncommon Passion. Read the biographies of men such as Thomas Edison, Thomas Jefferson or Napoleon. *They were consumed and obsessed.* It burned within them...*like fire.* Nothing else mattered to them but their goals and ambitions, right or wrong.

Passion Turns Common Men Into Uncommon Men.

3

THE PAIN OF YOUR PAST WILL DECIDE YOUR PASSION FOR YOUR FUTURE

Life Is The Survival Of Pain.

Your Memory Bank has stored one thousand painful moments, offenses, abuses and disappointments.

Most of these probably happened when you were a small child, incapable of defending yourself.

Nobody else has ever felt your pain.

Nobody.

Nobody is really concerned about your recovery, your comeback or your unspoken sorrow.

What can you do? Recognize that *Pain is the Factory for Energy, Force and Strength.*

Anger is simply passion requiring the correction of focus. You can turn your inner, hidden and deep pain as a Creative Force for Change, Ideas and incredible Productivity.

Your pain will start working for you...not against you.

Misfortune Is Always Temporary. Always.

So, do not adopt a belief system to explain away mediocrity, loss or even poverty. Wisdom Key: *Never*

Rewrite Your Theology To Accommodate A Tragedy. Your misfortune is only for a season.

Pain passes. The Laws of Life are permanent... and work when everything around you seems to fail.

Pain Is The Golden Bridge To Change. That is why you must view pain as the passage to promotion and change. "For His anger endureth but a moment; in His favour is life: weeping may endure for a night, but joy cometh in the morning," (Psalm 30:5).

My Personal Testimony

This happened to me many years ago. My world crashed. Suddenly, I was with a failed marriage, without a home, without inner hope...and without a penny in the bank.

Waves of hopelessness swept over me like ocean swells, leaving me confused and disheartened. *My passion for life and living were gone.* As my late friend, Jamie Buckingham, once said, "I didn't know *what* I believed. I only knew *in Whom* I believed." My recovery was lengthy, requiring many months of waiting on God and an intense search of the Scriptures before my life began to turn around.

A major decision was required and indescribably difficult to make. Should I forget my goals? Attempt to drop my dreams?

Or, should I fight back to ignite a spark of passion? My precious friend, please listen from your heart! Your future is your decision. Yours alone! Nobody else...NOBODY else is deciding your future. It is true: *If satan can steal your passion—he will destroy you and God's dream in you will die.*

Satan cannot steal your potential.

He can only steal your passion...for your future.

I must tell you, it was one of the most painful

battles in my entire life. The scars of my divorce were carved deep within me. I fought every demon in hell 24 hours a day. *Satan taunted me,* "You are an absolute failure. You are crazy if you think you will ever succeed in the ministry."

I read everything I could find.

I went to a variety of counselors.

I paid a fortune to Seminar Gurus.

Needing reassurance of God's call on my life, I read popular books by Christian counselors and even attended widely acclaimed seminars for help. These writers taught that ministers who failed in their marriages ought to leave the ministry and place themselves "on the shelf" for a time. This merely echoed what satan had already spoken to me. *I was tempted to agree.*

For I, too, had *always* wanted to be the *perfect* preacher, with a *perfect* wife and *perfect* children, doing *perfect* things.

I Wanted To Leave The Ministry

I began making plans to leave the ministry. I felt that God was through using me, and decided to go into business to support other preachers whom I admired...whom I thought were more "qualified" to represent the Gospel.

Yet, one nagging thought persisted. *I could not deny my calling, this inner anointing and passion to help heal broken lives.* I really cannot explain it. Even as I write these words I am overwhelmed with the memories of those emotions.

I kept *picturing* myself reaching out to broken-hearted, hurting people who were just like me... *stripped of their passion, bruised, fragmented...*people who desperately needed mending and reassurance of their worth.

Somehow, I knew that this ministry would be needed...*needed by those whose hearts had been torn and dreams ripped apart.*

Somebody...somewhere...needed what was within me.

No, God had never changed His original plan for me. Every demon in hell could not extract it from the soil of my spirit.

I decided to stay in the ministry. Regardless of the cost. Too many people were hurting just like me. Broken marriages and devastating financial setbacks have crushed the dreams of millions.

Slowly, the determination to fight back began to return. As my feelings poured from me, I penned songs such as, "You Can Make It," "God Will Outlast Your Storm," "He's A Healing Jesus," and my theme song, "I Want To Spend My Life Mending Broken People."

Can Lost Passion Return?

Slowly it began to happen. Those dark clouds surrounding my life began to vanish. *I recaptured my passion.*

The sun began to shine again.

My ministry weathered the storm and grew even *more effective* through the daily radio programs and weekly telecasts, "The Way Of The Winner," that eventually became known as "Wisdom Keys With Mike Murdock."

My Pain Birthed Uncommon Passion. Remember the woman at the well who hemorrhaged for twelve years..."And a certain woman, which had an issue of blood twelve years, And had suffered many things of many physicians, and had spent all that she had, and was nothing bettered, but rather grew worse," (Mark 5:25-26). Remember, too, the blind man who was no stranger to pain. "And it came to pass, that as He was come nigh unto Jericho, a certain blind man sat by the way side begging: And he cried, saying, Jesus, Thou Son of David, have mercy on me," (Luke 18:35, 38).

Every man fails. Champions simply get back up...and *begin again.* *Give God time to work.* Something good is happening that you do not yet see.

Wait joyfully with great expectation. "The Lord upholdeth all that fall, and raiseth up all those that be bowed down," (Psalm 145:14).

God has birthed these Uncommon Dreams within you...for a *reason.*

Somebody Is Waiting For You

Thousands can be healed through your restored passion. Have you heard about The Law of 250? I read some research on *The Circle of Influence*...that the average person influences 250 others. Those 250 influence another 250 each...confirming that our waves of influence are almost limitless.

Somebody broken...needs your passion.
Somebody confused...needs your passion.
Somebody hopeless...needs your passion.
*Somebody will fail...*unless *you* stay passionate.
*Somebody will commit suicide...*unless *you* stay passionate.

Should You Quit?

You may ask this question, *"Why* should I fight to stay passionate when it seems easier to stay depressed, uninvolved and just quit?"

Will quitting bring you *joy?* Then, quit.

Will quitting give you *peace?* Then, quit.

Will quitting remove your misery? Then, quit! But, think again. Think longer. Think honestly. *There is nothing to go back to. Quitting does not produce the desired result...so there is no reason to quit!*

Stop blaming painful childhood experiences.

Stop blaming your mate for all your feelings.

Stop waiting for everybody else to correct themselves...so you can experience a moment of enthusiasm and ecstasy.

Decide *now...*The Direction you want your life to go.

Decide *now...*The Environment you want to sculpture and customize for your Mind-World.

Decide *now...*what Success is to you and *you alone.*

Decide *now...*what you are willing to *live with...* and what you are unwilling to live without.

Choose what you want to experience.

Choose what you want to live around.

Choose the sounds that excite you.

Yesterday is over. Replaying it is ludicrous...and foolish.

Your Pain Is The Factory For Passion!

The Pain Of Your Past Will Decide Your Passion For Your Future.

❦ **4** ❦

TREASURE AND PROTECT YOUR FLOW OF PASSION

═══➤◗◦◖═══

It Happens To Everyone.

Your happiest moments *dissipate.*

Your passion and your energy suddenly dissolve... *in a moment.* You wake up one morning and the excitement to accomplishing *The Dream* is gone.

Your feelings are *not* your life.

Your feelings are...simply *feelings.*

Many people with *great potential* and *great dreams* have lost their passion to achieve them. Graveyards are filled with buried *dreams,* buried *treasures,* buried *possibilities...*that were never fulfilled.

They failed to protect their Passion.

You must learn the steps to take...what to do...when all the reasons, drive and passion for a worthwhile goal have dissipated.

Divorce can be *wrenching,* destroying all desire to live. *Loss of a loved one* can birth uncommon grief. *Disappointment* in a love relationship can make you literally want to die and wish you could disappear.

It is *possible* to regain lost passion. It is *necessary* to regain lost passion. *It is easier than you think...*to regain your passion.

You can dream...again. More effectively than ever.

4 Enemies To Your Passion

1. Fatigue Affects Your Passion. You can overwork yourself on a great and worthwhile dream. Fatigue and weariness of flesh can be devastating to a dream and a goal.

Tired Eyes Rarely See A Great Future.

When Fatigue Walks In, Faith Walks Out.

President Eisenhower would never make a major decision after a certain time in the afternoon. *Fatigue is an enemy to your passion. View* rest as an *achievement.* Even sleep is an *achievement!* Jesus instructed, "Come ye apart and rest a while," (see Mark 6:31).

God Himself rested on the seventh day after six days of creation. Was *He tired? Was His creativity exhausted?* Of course not. He knew...*the Rhythm of Life.*

2. Attempting Too Many Things At The Same Time Affects Your Passion. J. Paul Getty, the great billionaire, once said, "I've seen as many people fail from attempting too many things as attempting too few." Paul wrote, "This *one thing* I do," (Philippians 3:13). *Too many requirements* and demands on a doctor can result in a deterioration of *his own health.*

Overscheduled preachers, neglecting their own families, have experienced failed marriages *when they attempted to respond to the non-ending stream of requests piling high on their desk.*

Decide what matters the *most* to you.

Discern what matters *least.* Recognize your specific responsibilities to *God.* Pinpoint your responsibilities to your *family. Accept* your limitations. *Define* your frustrations. *Analyze* your observations.

Light the fires of passion again in your life.

3. Listening To Criticism Can Affect Your Passion. Has somebody lied about you? Have you been falsely accused? Has somebody written a terrible thing about you? *Do not allow anyone to dilute or dissolve your passion.*

One of the greatest teachers in our generation stated that he would not read bad reports about himself in the newspaper. He made this statement, "If you let it get in you, you now have the burden to get it out so you can get on with your life."

Your Success Is Determined By What You Are Willing To Ignore.

4. Unhealthy Relationships Affect Your Passion. Who *drains* you *emotionally?* Who has become a *parasite* in your financial life? Who is *disrespectful* in their conversations with you? *Every Friendship Does Not Have Equal Value.*

9 Ways To Recapture Your Lost Passion

1. Identify What Matters Most To The Heart Of God. What does God *expect* of you? What does God *require* of you? What has God *spoken* to you regarding your life? The Holy Spirit created you. *You are His greatest product.* The Holy Spirit is given to you so the desires of the Father...The Spirit..."that we might know the things that are freely given to us of God," (1 Corinthians 2:12). *He knows exactly where you belong.*

2. Identify What Matters The Most To You About Your Life. Your goals will continuously change. Stop pursuing dreams that no longer excite you. *Avoid* friendships that require unreasonable and exhausting labor and effort. "Have no fellowship with the unfruitful works of darkness, but rather reprove them," (Ephesians 5:11).

3.   Identify What Has Gone Wrong In Your Life. *Uncommon* Wisdom came from my *Uncommon* Mother regarding the will of God for my life. *"Son, the will of God is really an attitude, not a Place.* You can get in the will of God...in a single moment. The moment you recognize you are on the wrong track, cry out to God. Give Him your whole heart. At that moment, *when you surrender your whole heart to His plan and will, you will immediately enter and be in the center of the will of God."*

Those words have helped me beyond description. Your *past* can be *concluded*. Your *focus* can be *restored*. You can enter the perfect plan of God for your life...*in a single moment*.

4.   Identify The Specific Factors That Create Distraction And Loss Of Passion In Your Life. *Everything has a cause.* Known or not. Years ago, I wrote a song called, "There's A Reason For It All." The Bible says quite simply, "...the curse causeless shall not come," (Proverbs 26:2). *Identify Discouragers. Your Feelings Are Decided By Who You Have Chosen To Believe.*

5.   Recognize   Ingredients   In   The Atmosphere   That   Awaken   Your   Energy, Enthusiasm And Passion. For example, I love *learning. Knowledge unlocks me inside. Discovery is my greatest joy.*

The presence of God heals me inside. When I pray in The Secret Place, The Holy Spirit unlocks truths I never knew. My heart is awakened. My mind is on fire. *My goals become clear.*

The presence of God is invaluable to me.

6.   Identify Those Whose Conversations Unleash Your Passion.   *Words create currents.* Words create currents in your emotions, your home, your mind, your life and the very earth.   Words unleash war...or birth peace.

Words Are The Seeds For Feelings.

7.   Sing Songs Of Worship To Cure Deadly Introspection. *Worship will correct focus and bring you into the presence of God.*   "...come before His presence with singing," (Psalm 100:2). *The Holy Spirit will manifest His presence.*

8.   Learn Self-Talk To Encourage Yourself. *God gave you a mouth to conquer your mind.* "Let the words of my mouth, and the meditation of my heart, be acceptable in Thy sight, O Lord, My strength, and My redeemer," (Psalm 19:14).

9.   Choose   The   Vocabulary   Of   An Overcomer Instead Of A Victim.   Your words decide the You...others start seeing.   Words paint pictures in the minds of those around us.

Treasure And Protect Your Flow Of Passion.

What You Love
   To Learn About
Is A Clue To
   Your Passion.

-MIKE MURDOCK

❧ 5 ❧

WHAT YOU LOVE TO LEARN ABOUT MOST REVEALS YOUR PASSION

What You Love The Most Reveals You.

What do you love to *discuss?* What do you love to *hear about?* What *excites* you? These are clues to your passion, abilities and future. What You Love Is Where Your Wisdom Is. *You will always have Wisdom toward whatever you love.*

Great singers...love to sing. Teachers...love to teach. *What You Love To Learn About Is A Clue To Your Passion.*

Read everything you can about your *passion.*

Build the focus of your library around it.

7 Keys To Building Your Personal Wisdom Library Around Your Passion

1. Continuously Search For Books That Are Connected To Your Passion. You may find them in places you never dreamed. Used bookstores often have great purchases for just a few dollars.

Know what you truly enjoy. You alone can decide what generates *your* joy. Few friends will ever understand your unique *tastes, desires* and *excitements.*

2. Read For A Purpose. Read for *discovery.*

There is a place for passive and relaxed leisurely reading. Collect knowledge in a *special* notebook or computer.

3. Set Aside A Portion Of Your Monthly Budget For Wisdom You budget for electricity, food, clothes, insurance, housing and transportation. *You will not be able to pay for any of it without Wisdom!* Buy Wisdom.

4. Take A Speed-Reading Course. Invest in a speed-reading course. *Information is Strength.*

5. Establish A Separate Place Or Room As Your Personal "Wisdom Room." If it is a mere corner of a room, at least name it your "Wisdom Corner." *The Atmosphere You Create Determines The Product You Produce.*

6. Establish A Specific Time Each Day That You Listen To An Audio Book. Make your morning drive to work, "Automobile University." *Pay Any Price To Protect Your Focus And Keep It On Right Things.*

7. Use A Pink Highlighter Pen Continuously When You Read To Mark The Pages That Matter The Most. *Highlighting* enables effective reviewing.

Uncommon Achievers Always Consult Others. Learn from many. The Holy Spirit used forty different authors over a 1,600-year period to document Scriptures. Each author was inspired to focus on something different...*for a reason. Study* the lives of extraordinary and Uncommon Achievers. "...to know them which labour among you, and are over you in the Lord, and admonish you," (1 Thessalonians 5:12).

What You Love To Learn About Most Reveals Your Passion.

⁓ **6** ⁓

THOSE UNCOMFORTABLE WITH YOUR PASSION ARE UNQUALIFIED FOR INTIMACY

Intimacy Is Your Greatest Gift.

You must qualify others for intimate moments, conversations or knowledge.

Intimacy with *one wrong person* can destroy your passion forever. Wrong relationships will *weaken your passion* for your Assignment for God.

When God Wants To Bless You, He Brings A Person Into Your Life.

When Satan Wants To Destroy You, He Brings A Person Into Your Life.

Recently, I went to dinner with several friends after a church service. Within one hour, the discussion had become filled with the problems of people, financial difficulties and complaining attitudes. I was shocked at what began to grow within me. Though I had left the service with great joy, something *began to die* within me. I felt my own fire begin to go out. Paul warned of such associations. "Be not deceived: evil communications corrupt good manners," (1 Corinthians 15:33).

4 Questions That Qualify People For Intimacy

1. **Do They Love What You Do With Your**

Life?

2. What Questions Have They Asked That Reveal Their Passion To Adapt To Your Lifestyle?

3. What Price Are They Willing To Pay To Stay In Your Presence?

4. What Does It Take To Stop Them From Investing Their Life In Your Divine Assignment?

7 Important Reminders For Relationships

1. Intimacy Should Be Earned, Not Freely Given. *What You Respect, You Will Attract.* "…know them which labour among you, and are over you in the Lord, and admonish you; And to esteem them very highly in love for their work's sake," (1 Thessalonians 5:12-13).

2. Intimacy Should Be The Reward For Proven Loyalty And Respect. "Greater love hath no man than this, that a man lay down his life for his friends. Ye are My friends, if ye do whatsoever I command you," (John 15:13-14).

3. True Friendship Is A Gift, Never A Demanded Requirement. *A true friend will stay loyal, consistent during crisis.* True friends have the same enemies.

Your friend is always accessible during your times of loneliness. "A friend loveth at all times, and a brother is born for adversity," (Proverbs 17:17). Read the thirteenth chapter of First Corinthians.

4. When Wrong People Leave Your Life, Wrong Things Stop Happening. *Wrong People Birth Sad Seasons. Pursuers always have an Agenda and motive.* Spoken or not. Known or not. Pure or impure. Acceptable or unacceptable. Whatever the motive, uncover it…*whatever the cost.*

Remember the story of Jonah who was running from God's directive? "Wherefore they cried unto the Lord, and said, We beseech Thee, O Lord, we beseech Thee, let us not perish for this man's life, and lay not upon us innocent blood:...So they took up Jonah, and cast him forth into the sea: and the sea ceased from her raging," (Jonah 1:14-15).

5. **When Right People Enter Your Life, Right Things Begin To Happen.** "There cometh a woman of Samaria to draw water: Jesus saith unto her, Give Me to drink," (read John 4:7-15). *The briefest encounter in your life can be a golden link to the greatest dreams you have carried in your lifetime.* No relationship is insignificant. *Your Relationships Will Determine The Success Of Your Assignment. The Most Valuable Person In Your Life Is The One Who Feeds Your Faith.*

6. **If You Fail To Guard Your Own Life, You Are Like A City Without Walls.** "He that hath no rule over his own spirit is like a city that is broken down, and without walls," (Proverbs 25:28).

7. **Every Tragedy Begins With A Wrong Conversation.** Samson never forgot his introduction to Delilah. "And it came to pass afterward, that he loved a woman in the valley of Sorek, whose name was Delilah," (Judges 16:4).

*The Law of Eventuality...*is deciding your life.

Here Are 5 Important Keys To Help You When Someone Close To You Threatens To Break Your Focus From Your Passion

1. **Remember That God's Assignment For Your Life Is Permanent And Cannot Be Altered By Those Who Do Not Understand You.** There

will be moments in the pursuit of your Assignment when you feel *totally alienated* from those you love. It will appear they do not understand. It will seem that you alone are motivated to complete the instructions for your own life.

Isolation is more than emotional emptiness. It provokes absolute dependence upon The Holy Spirit. *It is during these times that you develop an addiction to His presence, His purpose, His plan and His power.*

2. Spend More Time In The Secret Place Hearing The Voice Of The Holy Spirit. "Call unto Me, and I will answer thee," (Jeremiah 33:3).

Private victories can birth *public* victories.

Private victories can lead to *public* honor.

3. Remember The Burning Divine Dream Within You. Joseph did. It was his Golden Secret for Survival. God will always fulfill His promise.

4. Reach For Intercessors. "..if two of you shall agree on earth as touching any thing that they shall ask, it shall be done for them of My Father which is in heaven," (Matthew 18:19).

5. Passionately Pursue Mentorship. Mentorship is Wisdom without the pain of waiting. Mentorship is learning from the pain another has experienced. Mentorship is the transfer of knowledge without the price of loss. "He that walketh with wise men shall be wise: but a companion of fools shall be destroyed," (Proverbs 13:20). *When you become obsessed in pursuing the right thing, wrong people will find you unbearable.*

You can lose in one day what took you twenty years to build. Do not risk it. Fight Any Battle Necessary To Maintain Your Focus And Keep Your Passion.

Those Uncomfortable With Your Passion Are Unqualified For Intimacy.

❧ 7 ❧

THE CROSS IS A PORTRAIT OF THE PASSION OF CHRIST

Passion Rules The Entire Earth.
The Passion Of Jesus Changed The World.
Jesus was passionate about *pleasing The Father.*
Jesus was passionate about *helping people.*
Jesus was passionate about *teaching protegés.*
Jesus was passionate about *learning.* He even pursued the mentorship of more experienced men...at the age of 12.

Jesus was a passionate Finisher. "I have glorified Thee on the earth: I have finished the work which Thou gavest Me to do," (John 17:4).

The Price God Was Willing To Pay Reveals The Worth Of The Product He Saw.

Jesus is our Supreme Example. As The Master Shepherd, He kept His passion alive through criticism, endless disrespect, hatred even when those nearest Him doubted His anointing and Assignment.

No Adversary Can Survive Your Passion. *So, ignite it...feed it...guard it...and expect it to penetrate any obstacle satan puts before you.*

Greater is He that is within me than he that is in

the world.

Something Inside You Is Stronger Than Anything Around You.

The Cross Is A Portrait Of The Passion Of Christ.

Our Prayer Together...

"Precious Heavenly Father,

...In The Name of Jesus, I receive a Heavenly Passion for Your Will and Assignment in my life.

...Your Passion is unleashed within me today.

...I accept a new Mantle and new Anointing for the new Season I am entering today.

...I will listen for Your Voice in The Secret Place...with Passion.

...I will follow Your Instructions with Passion.

...Ignite a new burning Passion to complete Your Divine Assignment in my life.

...I pray this in faith...In Jesus' name. Amen."

Precious Reader...

It is 1:11 a.m. as I finish this book...late Friday night. My heart longs to strengthen your hands, unlock the Treasure of your new season. Please know that the Prayer Team here at The Wisdom Center...will pray for you...over your personal letter or e-mail when you write. Simply e-mail...PrayNow@TheWisdomCenter.tv or call...817-759-0300 for an Intercessor during times of need.

We are here...because we care.

DR. MIKE MURDOCK

1 Has embraced his Assignment to Pursue...Proclaim...and Publish the Wisdom of God to help people achieve their dreams and goals.

2 Began full-time evangelism at the age of 19, which has continued since 1966.

3 Has traveled and spoken to more than 16,000 audiences in 39 countries, including East and West Africa, the Orient and Europe.

4 Noted author of over 200 books, including best sellers, *Wisdom for Winning*, *Dream Seeds* and *The Double Diamond Principle.*

5 Created the popular *Topical Bible* series for Businessmen, Mothers, Fathers, Teenagers; *The One-Minute Pocket Bible* series, and *The Uncommon Life* series.

6 The Creator of The Master 7 Mentorship System.

7 Has composed more than 5,700 songs such as "I Am Blessed," "You Can Make It," "God Rides On Wings Of Love" and "Jesus, Just The Mention Of Your Name," recorded by many gospel artists.

8 Is the Founder of The Wisdom Center, in Fort Worth, Texas.

9 Has a weekly television program called *Wisdom Keys With Mike Murdock.*

10 Has appeared often on TBN, CBN, BET and other television network programs.

11 Has had more than 3,000 accept the call into full-time ministry under his ministry.

THE MINISTRY

1 **Wisdom Books & Literature** - Over 200 best-selling Wisdom Books and 70 Teaching Tape Series.

2 **Church Crusades** - Multitudes are ministered to in crusades and seminars throughout America in "The Uncommon Wisdom Conferences." Known as a man who loves pastors he has focused on church crusades for 40 years.

3 **Music Ministry** - Millions have been blessed by the anointed songwriting and singing of Mike Murdock, who has made over 15 music albums and CDs available.

4 **Television** - *Wisdom Keys With Mike Murdock,* a nationally-syndicated weekly television program.

5 **The Wisdom Center** - The Church and Ministry Offices where Dr. Murdock speaks weekly on Wisdom for The Uncommon Life.

6 **Schools of The Holy Spirit** - Mike Murdock hosts Schools of The Holy Spirit in many churches to mentor believers on the Person and Companionship of The Holy Spirit.

7 **Schools of Wisdom** - In many major cities Mike Murdock hosts Schools of Wisdom for those who want personalized and advanced training for achieving "The Uncommon Dream."

8 **Missions Outreach** - Dr. Mike Murdock's overseas outreaches to 39 countries have included crusades in East and West Africa, South America, the Orient and Europe.

The Businessman's Devotional Book Pak!

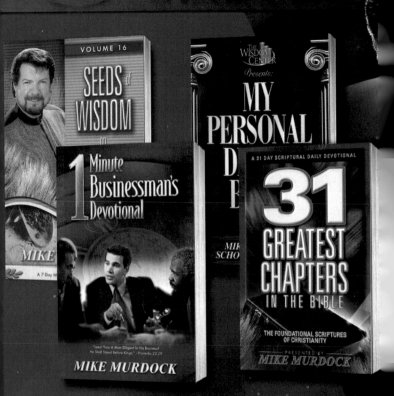

1 Seeds of Wisdom on Problem-Solving/<u>Book</u> (32pg/B-

2 My Personal Dream Book/<u>Book</u> (32pg/B-143/$5)

3 1 Minute Businessman's Devotional
/<u>Book</u> (224pg/B-42/$12)

4 31 Greatest Chapters In The Bible
/<u>Book</u> (138pg/B-54/$10)

The Wisdo...
Th...
Businessma...
tional 4 B...
Only $2...
PAK...
Wisdom Is The...

*Each Wisdom Book may be purchased separately if so desired.

Add 10%...

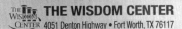

The Businesswoman's Devotional
Book Pak!

❶ Seeds of Wisdom on Problem-Solving /Book (32pg/B-118/$5)

❷ My Personal Dream Book/Book (32pg/B-143/$5)

❸ 1 Minute Businesswoman's Devotional
/Book (224pg/B-43/$12)

❹ 31 Greatest Chapters In The Bible
/Book (138pg/B-54/$10)

*Each Wisdom Book may be purchased separately if so desired.

The Wisdom Center
The Businesswoman's Devotional 4 Book Pak!
Only **$20** $32 Value
PAK-33
Wisdom Is The Principal Thing

Add 10% For S/H

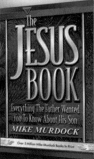
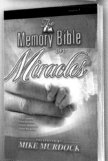
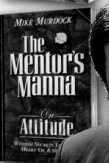

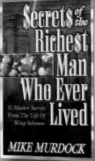

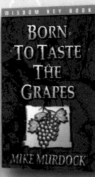

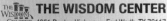

Career 7

Book Pak For Business People!

DR. MIKE MURDOCK

❶ **The Businessman's Topical Bible**/Book (384pg/B-33/$10)

❷ **31 Secrets for Career Success**/Book (114pg/B-44/$10)

❸ **31 Scriptures Every Businessman Should Memorize**/Book (32pg/B-141/$3)

❹ **Seeds of Wisdom on Goal-Setting**/Book (32pg/B-127/$5)

❺ **Seeds of Wisdom on Problem-Solving**/Book (32pg/B-118/$5)

❻ **Seeds of Wisdom on Productivity**/Book (32pg/B-137/$5)

❼ **The Mentor's Manna on Achievement**/Book (32pg/B-79/$3)

The Wisdom Center
Career 7 Book Pak!
Only $30
$41 Value
WBL-27
Wisdom Is The Principal Thing

Add 10% For S/H

Each Wisdom Book may be purchased separately if so desired.

F

 THE WISDOM CENTER 4051 Denton Highway • Fort Worth, TX 76117

1-817-759-BOOK
1-817-759-0300

You Will Love Our Website...!
TheWisdomCenter.tv

Spirit Music.

The Mike Murdock Music Library

LOVE SONGS TO THE HOLY SPIRIT

Written In The Secret Place

TS-59

DR. MIKE MURDOCK

THE HOLY SPIRIT HANDBOOK

What You Need To Know About Your Daily Companion, The Holy Spirit

Songs...

1. A Holy Place
2. Anything You Want
3. Everything Comes From You
4. Fill This Place With Your Presence
5. First Thing Every Morning
6. Holy Spirit, I Want To Hear You
7. Holy Spirit, Move Again
8. Holy Spirit, You Are Enough
9. I Don't Know What I Would Do Without You
10. I Let Go (Of Anything That Stops Me)
11. I'll Just Fall On You
12. I Love You, Holy Spirit
13. I'm Building My Life Around You
14. I'm Giving Myself To You
15. I'm In Love! I'm In Love!
16. I Need Water (Holy Spirit, You're My Well)
17. In The Secret Place

18. In Your Presence, I'm Always Changed
19. In Your Presence (Miracles Are Born)
20. I've Got To Live In Your Presence
21. I Want To Hear Your Voice
22. I Will Do Things Your Way
23. Just One Day At A Time
24. Meet Me In The Secret Place
25. More Than Ever Before
26. Nobody Else Does What You Do
27. No No Walls!
28. Nothing Else Matters Anymore (Since I've Been In The Presence Of You Lord)
29. Nowhere Else
30. Once Again You've Answered
31. Only A Fool Would Try (To Live Without You)
32. Take Me Now
33. Teach Me How To Please You

34. There's No Place I'd Rather Be
35. Thy Word Is All That Matters
36. When I Get In Your Presence
37. You're The Best Thing (That's Ever Happened To Me)
38. You Are Wonderful
39. You've Done It Once
40. You Keep Changing Me
41. You Satisfy

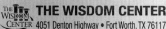

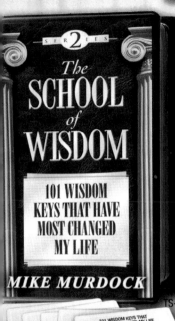
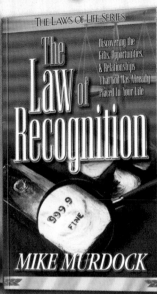

Financial $ecrets

31 REASONS PEOPLE DO NOT RECEIVE THEIR **FINANCIAL HARVEST** — MIKE MURDOCK

The Wisdom Center
Buy One... Receive The Second One FREE!
Wisdom Is The Principal Thing

VIDEO
7 KEYS to 1000 TIMES MORE
The Lord God Of Your Fathers Make You A Thousand Times So Many More As You Are, And Bless You, As He Hath Promised You! Deuteronomy 1:11
MIKE MURDOCK

Your Financial World Will Change Forever.

Video 2-Pak!

▶ 8 Scriptural Reasons You Should Pursue Financial Prosperity

▶ The Secret Prayer Key You Need When Making A Financial Request To God

▶ The Weapon Of Expectation And The 5 Miracles It Unlocks

▶ How To Discern Those Who Qualify To Receive Your Financial Assistance

▶ How To Predict The Miracle Moment God Will Schedule Your Financial Bre
through

▶ Habits Of Uncommon Achievers

▶ The Greatest Success Law I Ever Discovered

▶ How To Discern Your Place Of Assignment,
The Only Place Financial Provision Is Guaranteed

▶ 3 Secret Keys In Solving Problems For Others

The Wisdom Center
Video 2-Pak!
Only **$30** $60 Value
VIPAK-01
Wisdom Is The Principal Thing

Add 10% For S/H

Favor 4!

The SCHOOL of WISDOM · 31 KEYS TO UNLEASHING UNCOMMON FAVOR · MIKE MURDOCK

The Pastoral Collection of Mike Murdock · The Hidden Power Of Right Words · VOLUME 27 · FREE BOOK ENCLOSED

SEEDS of WISDOM on FAVOR · VOLUME 17 · MIKE MURDOCK

This Collection Of Wisdom Will Change The Seasons Of Your Life Forever!

SEEDS of WISDOM · Mike Murdock · VOLUME 8 · on OBEDIENCE

1 The School of Wisdom #4 / 31 Keys To Unleashing Uncommon Favor...Tape Series/6 Cassettes (TS-44/$30)

2 The Hidden Power Of Right Words... The Wisdom Center Pastoral Library/CD (WCPL-27/$10)

3 Seeds of Wisdom on Favor/Book (32pg/B-119/$5)

4 Seeds of Wisdom on Obedience/Book (32pg/B-20/$3)

*Each Wisdom Product may be purchased separately if so desired.

The CRISIS COLLECTION

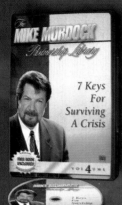

You Get All 6 For One Great Price!

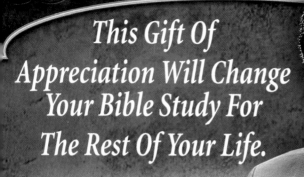

This Gift Of Appreciation Will Change Your Bible Study For The Rest Of Your Life.

The Wisdom Bible

MY GIFT OF APPRECIATION

Celebrating Your Sponsorship Seed of $1,000 For The Prayer Center & TV Studio Complex

B-235

Wisdom Is The Principal Thing

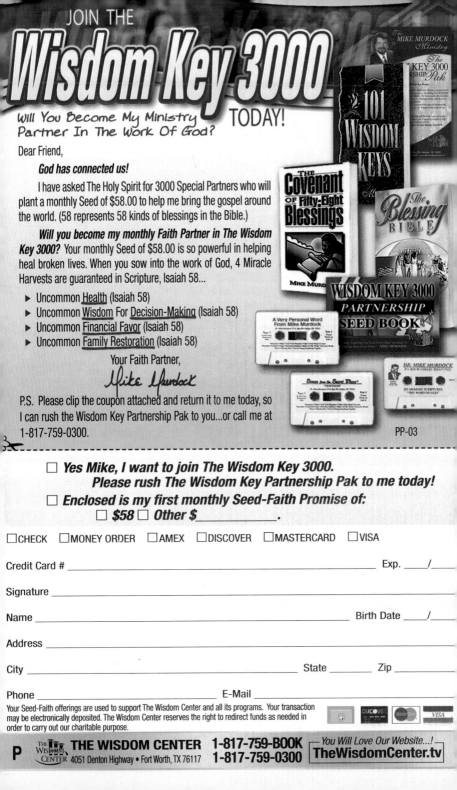

JOIN THE
Wisdom Key 3000
TODAY!

Will You Become My Ministry Partner In The Work Of God?

Dear Friend,

God has connected us!

I have asked The Holy Spirit for 3000 Special Partners who will plant a monthly Seed of $58.00 to help me bring the gospel around the world. (58 represents 58 kinds of blessings in the Bible.)

Will you become my monthly Faith Partner in The Wisdom Key 3000? Your monthly Seed of $58.00 is so powerful in helping heal broken lives. When you sow into the work of God, 4 Miracle Harvests are guaranteed in Scripture, Isaiah 58...

▶ Uncommon <u>Health</u> (Isaiah 58)
▶ Uncommon <u>Wisdom</u> For <u>Decision-Making</u> (Isaiah 58)
▶ Uncommon <u>Financial Favor</u> (Isaiah 58)
▶ Uncommon <u>Family Restoration</u> (Isaiah 58)

Your Faith Partner,

Mike Murdock

P.S. Please clip the coupon attached and return it to me today, so I can rush the Wisdom Key Partnership Pak to you...or call me at 1-817-759-0300.

PP-03

☐ **Yes Mike, I want to join The Wisdom Key 3000.**
Please rush The Wisdom Key Partnership Pak to me today!

☐ **Enclosed is my first monthly Seed-Faith Promise of:**
☐ **$58** ☐ **Other $_____.**

☐CHECK ☐MONEY ORDER ☐AMEX ☐DISCOVER ☐MASTERCARD ☐VISA

Credit Card # _____ Exp. ____/____

Signature _____

Name _____ Birth Date ____/____

Address _____

City _____ State _____ Zip _____

Phone _____ E-Mail _____

Your Seed-Faith offerings are used to support The Wisdom Center and all its programs. Your transaction may be electronically deposited. The Wisdom Center reserves the right to redirect funds as needed in order to carry out our charitable purpose.

THE WISDOM CENTER 4051 Denton Highway • Fort Worth, TX 76117

1-817-759-BOOK
1-817-759-0300

You Will Love Our Website...!
TheWisdomCenter.tv